Where Did You Go?
A 21st Century Guide to
Finding Yourself Again

Andrew Brechko

WHERE DID YOU GO?

A 21ST CENTURY GUIDE TO FINDING YOURSELF AGAIN

ANDREW BRECHKO

© 2017 by Andrew Brechko

Printed in the United States of America
First Printing, 2017

Rusty Wheels Media, LLC.
P.O. Box 1692
Rome, GA 30162

ISBN-13: 978-0692831465
ISBN-10: 0692831460
Printed in the United States of America

Mom and Dad: I am incredibly lucky to have parents as amazing as you.

Grandma: Thanks for always loving my adventurous ways. Here's to the author in all of us.

My English Teachers Mrs. Royer and Mrs. Collins: You read everything I wrote and always smiled. Your comments didn't only impact my grade, they impacted my life.

CONTENTS

CHAPTER 1

A NEW BEGINNING

If you are satisfied with living according to the status quo, in a state of mediocrity, this book is not for you. If you are not willing to work, make difficult choices about your time, relationships, and life focus to enhance your existence, please put this book back on the shelf. If you are perfectly content to let every day pass you by, knowing that you want to do something great, but have no intention to give action to that inner voice, this book is not for you. Finally, if you are not willing to feel a little discomfort in order to bring about incredible positive change in your life, stop reading now.

If you feel like there is more to life than what you are living, this book is for you. If you feel like there is something inside of you that is struggling to get out, this book is for you. If you are ready to make a major life change in order to live an epic existence based on passion, success, and fulfillment, this book is for you. If you want to have an incredible amount of positive impact on yourself, your closest friends, your family and ultimately the world…this book is for you!

Although this journey is about finding the true you, it is not a self-centered approach to life. Living a self-centered life can be very harmful to our emotional well-being. We are community creatures, and focusing solely on oneself is detrimental to our growth. The strategies in this book are designed to make you a better, happier person who enjoys life at a higher level. This, in turn, has a positive effect on your relationships, your workplace, your community, and on the world. Every one of us has our ups and downs in life. That is how it always has been and always will be. Every day will not be perfect. When you live true to yourself and allow the truth to shine out, the ups and the downs will be much easier to manage. Your life will begin to take on a new meaning. You will look forward to greeting each day in the morning and will celebrate when it is finished.

I tend to be very honest, straightforward, and to the point. My hope is that this book encourages and inspires as many people as possible to move into the realm of a happy life, an amazing life. That is who I am. This will be no easy task for you, just as it is not been an easy task for me to get where I am. If you are not up to the challenge, close this book. If you are ready, read on.

Finding the true you and making the changes in your life does require hard work, dedication, and resiliency. If you want it though, it can be yours. I don't sugar coat things very much, so if my statements to you are a bit brusque yet poignant, it is because I want you to be better and truer to yourself and therefore live the rest of your life like you have never lived it before. Live a life full of experience, adventure, excitement, love, passion, and happiness.

We are all on a journey here, regardless of your beliefs which revolve around religion, race, ethnicity, your job, your age, height, weight, or sex. Here are some things that hold true throughout our existence:

1. We were all born

2. We are all weird or abnormal

3. We all want to be happy

4. We all have talents and gifts

5. We will all die

These are all guarantees, but no matter what we do, you and I will share both one and five. My question to you is: what are you going to do with your life between one and five? This book is about two through four and is dedicated to a life that is lived being true to whoever you are. The world craves originality. Those who are the most successful, happy, influential and inspiring are the most original. Once you rediscover yourself and let your inner "you" shine out, there is no telling what great things will come your way. I want the time between one and five to count for you, so that when you hit number five, you can leave with a smile.

Embrace who you are and use it to your strengths. Maybe you are an incredible worker, a great singer, are driven to build a successful business, want to create an organization that helps people, want to become a teacher, an artist, a musician. The list goes on. You have a desire and this inner desire is the true "you" fighting to get out. Don't you think it is about time to let it soar?

Some of you may feel like you fall outside of the realm of normal. You look at the world and you say, everybody else is doing awesome, but why am I struggling so much? I have so many issues from my past and present. It is just unfair. My response is that everyone has trouble, often viewing themselves as inadequate or abnormal. So what is normal? This question seems very easy on the surface. Upon further examination, we find it a bit more difficult to answer.

I am not normal and there is a good chance that you are not normal either. This is not to say that you are a freak, but we are all individuals living on this planet and being an individual, being unique, is one of the most powerful things we possess. This holds especially true because we live in a free, democratic nation that allows us to take advantage of our own personal talents, desires, and passions. Why then are so many people locked in their own misery? This is because they are trying to live in this concept of normal which suppresses their true individualism and its ability to come into the world. I do not believe there is such thing as normal and the sooner you realize that the sooner you will be able to begin your journey to true happiness.

What you have been made to think normal or acceptable is a societal human design brought to you by enormous and ever-powerful media machines. They make their money by making you feel like you are abnormal, inadequate, and set the ever changing target for normal based on a new product, a new TV series, or a new clothing line. Although I am thankful that I am able to enjoy the amazing benefits of the 21st century, some of which include great beer, fantastic coffee and internet radio, the personal pitfalls created by these benefits are immense, but not insurmountable. I believe that every person can rise against the machine and be themselves; all the while adding tremendous worth to family, friends, work and the world.

CHAPTER 2

MY STORY

So what qualifies me to write this book and why should you listen to me? First, I know exactly how it feels to live a life just on the outside of what normal is supposed to be. Over the years I have struggled to allow my true self to take control and be my guide. The past few years, I have given my true self more power in my path in life. I felt like it was time to write a book for those millions of people like me who feel that their true self is trapped, just waiting to get out. This is not an easy process by any means, but the rewards are incredible.

How can you spot an individual that is living their life according to their true nature, personality, and passions? Look at their smile. That will tell you everything you need to know. I have struggled with being me my entire life and it wasn't until I began this book that I actually have come to grips with my personality, decisions, and desires. This has allowed me to make some unapologetic decisions that have really driven me to go after my passions. This tactic is not easy, it takes enormous courage to take the plunge, but it is worth it. Let me retrace my route for you.

For most of my life, I have been called weird, crazy, out of control, etc. When I was in elementary school and middle school, I was an incessant talker and would never shut up. I often disrupted classes and was considered the class clown. I loved to make people laugh and although I did spend quite a bit of time being yelled at by my teachers and even my principle, I was well liked by almost all of my teachers and peers. It was often stated that I walked to the beat of a different drum. At times, I wish that I was normal like the other cool kids. Some nights, I would make a conscious decision to go to school the next day and try to mirror the popular kids. I tried to suppress my inner self. The attempt would last for a few days, and slowly I drifted back to my old habits because my inner self was so powerful, it refused to be constrained. If I was quiet, students and parents would ask me if I was feeling ok and after a while, I realized that I was expected to be my energetic, spirited, comical character by everyone.

This side of me was very different from the rest of my brothers and sisters. Why, I wondered? For starters, I am one of six children, located second to last in my family. Psychologists, love to attribute behavior to birth order. For me, that would mean rebellious. Although I do believe in the great work psychologists do, I am hesitant to allow blanket diagnosis define my destiny. It would be easy to defer blame of my different behaviors and character traits for my failure or success in life, but I am not a big believer in molds. Actually, I prefer to break them. I have learned that I am who I am, and you are who you are. Don't apologize for this-Ever. Of course, I can make these statements twenty-two years out of high school. High school was a bit of a challenge with my weird personality. It wasn't until I was out of the public education system that my personality traits actually proved to be a benefit rather than a burden. I was often asked by the teachers, who also taught my siblings, why I couldn't be more like them. All of my other siblings were very good students and in many cases were quiet in class. I didn't have a good answer for the teachers or the principal except to explain to them the fact that I was not my brothers or sister.

Interestingly enough, there was a point in my high school career that changed my life. My brother Jason, who is next older than myself was telling me about an English course named Creative Writing.

"Gosh," I said to him, "That sounds incredibly boring!" as I began to walk away.

He said, "Well, the cool thing about it is you can write about whatever you want and you can swear!"

Of course, that got my attention as I turned around, my curiosity peaked, "swear and write about whatever I want?" I asked.

"Yep," he replied.

"I am all in," I told him and signed up for the course the next year.

He was right, we could write about whatever we wanted and I took full advantage. I tried to write the most outrageous things and my teacher never lost her cool, always laughed and continued on. I never got under her skin, which was always a game for me…student vs. teacher! Please see rebellious in the above family positioning paragraph.

One of the last projects we had to do was to write a short story. This was my chance to really go off the wall. The name of the story was *Jon-Jon Walters*. This still lives in a legendary status among both my classmates and my teacher. I pulled out all stops, pushing the limits of "creativity" as best as I could as I produced this literary masterpiece. As it turned out, *Jon-Jon Walters* would change my life. In retrospect, I probably should have seen a counselor or something and today I am sure that I would be immediately escorted to the school psychologist for an evaluation.

I submitted the piece of literary genius on time to my teacher and stated with a big smile, "enjoy!" and walked to my seat. I was eager for the outcome and waited a few days for the story to be graded and returned to us. The day came and I was expecting the teacher to have a bigger response, I mean, this was a very creative story. As always, she didn't show a response. She passed them out and placed the short story with a big C on top, and in red she wrote, "You need to channel your humor." "Channel my humor", I thought, "that is crazy!" This was supposed to be creative writing. This was a true work of literary genius so, of course, I had to challenge her. The teacher explained that my paper was far too crazy, she even let her husband read it and they both agreed that I needed to channel my humor.

What did this mean, "channel my humor?" She explained that I was intelligent, creative and had a great sense of humor but if I didn't control it, I would struggle in life. I thought my sense of humor was perfectly fine and waltzed out the door when the bell rang.

That phrase kept returning to me over the next couple months. Was she right, did I need to channel my humor, or more constructively put, channel my energy? Dang it, I hate when other people are right about me. This was one of those small moments, a series of words in this case, that changed my life. If I wasn't able to channel my energy to productive means I would end up going through life annoying everyone with my humor and not able to get my dreams and goals accomplished.

So this became my grounding rod, to "channel my humor". In this case, this was my sense of self, but I would need to try to take my energy and focus. I slowly learned how to control myself and little by little, I was able to reign myself in and focus on my goals. Of course, this isn't to say that I would lose control of my "humor" as I finished high school and entered college.

There may or may not have been a bottle of

Southern Comfort under the seat of my car for my early morning philosophy class, or a water bottle that was a perfect disguise for vodka, there is also a possibility that I was asked to leave a couple of lecture halls by the professor. All in all, I pulled through and by "channeling my humor" I ended up graduating from my community college with a 3.7.

The real honing of my energy came when I joined the military after I graduated community college. Let's just say that my drill sergeants didn't appreciate a little private with a sense of humor. I learned that there are times to speak and times to keep my trap shut. I began to exercise as a way to burn off my energy and began to learn that if I added structure to my life, which Uncle Sam does a great job of; I was able to accomplish my goals over time. "Man," I would always think to myself, "this channeling my humor thing actually works."

In addition to the structure of the military, I also was exposed to many different people from many different walks of life. I loved to learn where people came from, but more importantly I embraced their different perspectives. These associations taught me a lot and increased my breadth of knowledge. Being around soldiers also inspired me to go after my dreams. In case you didn't know, the military doesn't necessarily draw from the top levels of society. In many cases with the people I served with, the military was their only way out of their circumstance, which was typically poverty. In many cases when compared to their family and friends, they were the first and only ones with high school and college degrees, the only ones not to have run in's with the law or serve time in prison, the only ones who were not addicts, and the only ones with a stable job. In other words, the only ones who had made it. They were and continue to be true mold breakers, and I continue to be in awe of their tenacity, pride, and successes.

My military service was full of challenges, life lessons, and structure, which I didn't always agree with. I did my share of physical labor after duty hours and extracurricular exercise for talking back and being a little rambunctious. Yet through it all, I was able to maintain my uniqueness and closely connected to my true self. I began to see the value in my happiness as I was able to maintain positive social relationships, command the respect of my peers and employers, as well as feel free to go after my dreams and passions.

As I have harnessed my uniqueness and allowed my true self to be free, with encouraging and positive results, I began to think about everyone else's struggles with rediscovering who they are. So many people in our society today put on fake smiles to their loved ones, their friends and acquaintances, yet have a deep desire to allow their true self to come out. Remember, you only have one time around on this rock and you need to use it appropriately. At the end of this journey, there are no re-dos! Regrets can never be addressed and redone. This book is designed for those people who want to throw off the chains of normalcy and live a life true to them by allowing their true selves to thrive in the world.

If you are ready, read on. This is a journey that is not an easy one, yet the most rewarding experiences of life will happen when you change the way that you live to one that is true to your "you". There is only one person who can make this change and that is you! In life, there are talkers and doers. There are those who pay lip service to make changes and desperately want to retake control of their lives. They often stay in the same place because they don't have the courage to take the serious steps required to rediscover their true selves and allow it to come out.

These are the talkers. At first, they are good to be around, but then you find out that they are a drain because they never move forward, it becomes a groundhog day, every day. They make the same mistakes, same choices and complain about how unfair the world is. Well, this book isn't for talkers, it is for doers. Doers and talkers have the same dreams, goals, and aspirations. The difference is that doers actually have the courage to take the steps to bring about the positive change they want in their lives as well as the world. They set goals, they "channel their humor" they allow their "you" to bring about what they want.

If you are reading this book, you are ready for a positive change. This is the first step in a long, exciting journey. So how is this book going to help you find your "you"? Simple, this book is full of insights, thought-provoking questions, viewpoints, and suggestions. I want you to cut your own path and these writings will help. My path and yours are different, we live on our own side of normal, but our goals are the same. We both want to be happy and healthy (mentally, spiritually, physically, and emotionally). We want to find fulfillment, we want to let our true selves shine through and we want to live a life that enables us to follow our dreams, desires, and passions. After all, life is short, and you can rest when you are dead!

CHAPTER 3

YOU ARE MEANT TO DO SOMETHING IMPORTANT

Have you ever quieted your mind and listened to your heart, to your soul, to your thoughts? It's in these moments, where you can hear the faint cries of the inner "you" trying to come out. You know this needs to be freed, but you use your situation, your logical mind to keep it from spreading its wings and flying. You can keep it caged if you prefer, but imagine what good it would do for the world if you set it free.

I believe that we were all put on this earth to do something. At this point in time, there are 7.3 billion of us. Think about that for a second. That is an enormous amount of potential. Now, imagine if every person in the world lived a life true to their gifts, their talents, and their abilities to make the world a better place. Now think about the fact that each and every single one of us has a talent to offer.

So here is a hard hitting question…what do you have to offer and do you have the courage to offer it?

We live in a time with so much technological and social influence that we often feel like we are small and what we have to offer isn't much. It is very easy to get lost in the noise of social media, the internet, and advertising. With the volume turned all the way up in what seems like 24/7. This can very easily drown out your voice. It can rob you of your forward progress, your desires, and your motivation. To combat this pressure you need to turn it down and your "you" up. Each person has something this world can benefit from, including you. What you have to offer to the world is incredibly valuable. So valuable that you can't put a price tag on it. Your gifts are so unique, so special, and powerful they must be shared.

You will blush and say that what you have to offer isn't that important and I must stop that thought right there. It is crucial to yourself and to the world that you share what you have. If you take your gift with you when you die, it will never get the chance to make a positive change in the world.

"But so many people are naturally gifted," you may say to yourself. Yes, there are many people who have extraordinary gifts. When we look at them we don't see the time, effort and struggles they dedicated to honing their gift so that it can be let out into the world. These people are passed off as an overnight success, a quick turnaround, or are even just lucky.

In 2008 Malcolm Gladwell wrote a booked titled *Outliers*. In his book, he makes the argument that it takes 10,000 hours to develop expertise at anything. Although this theory is contested and touted as an oversimplification of success, I think his theory is relevant to use in this case. People who achieve success using their gifts realize the path they must take. Their gift is their guide, they rise with it, fall with it, learn from it, and let it guide them. They hone it, alter it, they use it both as a teacher and as a student and after hours of practice with it, they eventually benefit from their gift. Every single person who has benefitted from their natural gift has made enormous sacrifices in order to benefit from it. They kept their earphones in when the noise of comparison, critique, and naysaying became loud. They tried a thousand times and failed, only to try one more time to discover success. This is what it takes. Regardless of age, your successes are only ahead, especially if you live true to your calling and you focus on releasing it into the world. Rediscovering your true you can be comparable to this process. It requires your full attention, dedication, and focus.

One of the traps that people fall into when they get older is they feel like they don't deserve to be happy. As adults, we sometimes believe that our ship has sailed, that the change in this book is for the young, the uninhibited, those without the responsibilities that adult life brings. This became apparent in a conversation I was having with a close friend named Kayte. I asked her how life was going and I got a depressed response. She explained that she was "trying to figure out what she wanted to be when she grew up." I need to mention that Kayte was 48 years old. I asked her why she was so depressed. She stated that she felt lesser than her peers because they appeared to be so successful, were confident in their careers, their family life, and their personal growth. This type of comparison can rob you of your motivation to rediscover yourself. There are many people in the world who find themselves in the same situation as Katye. They just don't have the courage to admit it or to do something about it. It can seem like a daunting task to make a change in life after you worked so hard only to find out that you may have made a wrong career choice at the age of 18 when you chose your path.

There is good news though. Finding your true you and living a life you love doesn't always require you to turn your life upside down, quit your job, or make a drastic life change. What it does require you to do is examine what your inner voice is saying to you. There is a very key point here that I need to mention early in this book. Life is about positioning (there is a whole chapter dedicated to this later, so read on). Sometimes we have to spend years to create the circumstance that would allow our true selves to come out. Often though, it is as simple as taking art or dance class, buying an old car and fixing it up, getting a degree in something that you love, starting a full time or part time business, learning to ride a horse, creating something amazing and beautiful, going on a big adventure or a series of small ones, the list goes on and on. Our true selves are so diverse. I believe that whatever your path to fulfillment is, you can start by examining the issues I write about in this book. Your transformation is possible and it is close. Begin to look inward and visualize what this change will look like. If you follow your calling, your happiness and fulfillment level will increase tenfold.

CHAPTER 4

TO BE YOURSELF IS TO BE THE HAPPIEST PERSON ON EARTH

What does it mean to be happy? Are normal people happy? Can I be happy if I am not considered normal? These are questions often asked by all of us throughout all our lives. I often hear this "happiness" word thrown around in our society all the time. In the industrialized world, you can see the concept of happiness, not in the smile or laughter generated by people, but in advertisements, commercials, and on the internet. The odd thing is that whenever you see this happiness, there is a product to go along with it and you are not happy until you have this new gadget.

Imagine a new product that featured an overweight couple, with disheveled appearances and major frowns saying, "We love this product and so will you!" Absolutely not. This isn't how advertising works. The secret to get you to buy a product or service is to make you feel inadequate, and the only way that you will feel adequate is if you purchase said product or service. This, of course, isn't to say that you should stop buying things, but just be aware of where you are looking for your happiness.

It is interesting when I hear older couples talk about their happiest times together. It is usually when they first got together and they didn't have a pot to pee in or two nickels to rub together. They were usually at a phase in their lives where they were just trying to make ends meet in a relationship that was not clouded by pursuing material things or paying off debt. They were able to enjoy the little things in life and to spend quality time with each other. In the industrialized world, we seem to incessantly chase this concept called happiness and rightfully so.

In the small nation of Bhutan, there is actually a Gross National Happiness (GNH) Index that measures the nation's happiness level. You can check it out on their website www.grossnationalhappiness.com. The king of Bhutan came up with the concept in the 1970's. The idea behind measuring a nation's happiness gave value to the emotional well-being of his population. The concept of GNH is measured in conjunction with the monetary success of a nation or the Gross Domestic Product. GNH was a revolutionary idea which has gained notoriety since Bhutan adopted it over 40 years ago. The idea of measuring people's happiness became so important that in 2011, the United Nations passed Resolution 65/309. This resolution gave weight to the importance of a society's happiness as another way to measure a nation's social and economic development.

Happiness is important to us. If you search the word *happiness* in books on Amazon the result is over 100,000. So this bears the question, if we have such a high standard of living then why do we chase happiness?

In the world of capitalism, we are taught to equate happiness with money, but the reality is that one does not need a ton of money to be happy. "What?" you ask, "No...that can't be true!" Well, it is true, sort of. Money is only a small ingredient in the pie of happiness. A study in 2010, by Daniel Kahneman (a psychologist) and Angus Deaton (an economist) came to the conclusion that any income over $75,000 per year does not significantly increase a person's happiness by that much. True?...maybe.

The correlations between money and happiness can be very abstract and arbitrary. We like to think that the relationship is direct. If only I had this, I would be happy or look at that guy in the Ferrari or the girl who always dresses in designer clothes, she/he must be happy. I think that it depends on more than just the concept that every dollar you make, your happiness will increase by that percentage. In my life, I have met my share of miserable million-aires, granted they were miserable over different things than what a miserable person in poverty would be miserable about, but nonetheless, they were miserable and miserable is miserable! (That is seven miserables in one sentence…that is a whole lot of misery).

So the real key to understanding, getting, being, and sustaining happiness is to look at the interconnected relationships between happiness and life. It is not a linear chart with direct relationships like you would see in a standard study. For example, an increase in salary results in a direct increase in happiness. Happiness is more like a convoluted, twisted relationship with life that has constant changing inputs. It has to do with our souls, our relationships, allowing our "you" to come out. Are we living a fulfilled life? It would be silly for me to think that a single book would eliminate society's quest for material things to increase happiness, but I do think that we can do a better job of how we spend our money on things that will make us happy. When we examine what a happiness formula should look like, I have to add a word of caution, and a trap that I fell into myself. It goes like this: Do I love something, or do I just love the thought of it?

Let me give you an example: I like old VW's and I would picture myself driving in a 1976 Westfalia (camper van), rolling up a curvy road on my way to a music festival. The windows would be down and the wind would blow through my long hair (which is really a pipe dream considering my male pattern baldness). I would be going slower than traffic and there would be a line of cars behind me, but they wouldn't mind because the van was super cool. I would get to the campsite, pop the top on both the van and a beer and listen to the bands play as people would walk by and say, "cool van man," and I would reply with an ever so confident hippy response, "thanks, dude!" So, that would be the *I love the thought of it.*

In reality, I did buy a 1976 VW Westfalia and the *I love thought of it* wore away on the side of a highway in Vermont as the van broke down. Turns out, people don't really think hippy vans are that cool because no one even slowed to 80mph when passing me laying under the van with my arm in a sling after my shoulder surgery and gasoline running down my face. The reality became real. I loved the thought of it, but I hated to work on old vehicles. Needless to say, my dreams ended then and there and the van never ran again (I am not a master mechanic). Eventually, the van was sold to a guy who loved it, he eventually fixed it and is living the dream somewhere, at least I hope so. The van was a better idea in my mind. Now, before I ever take those leaps into forays of adventure, I always ask the vital question...Do I love it, or do I just love the thought of it?

Your happiness state is different than mine and both are based on our core personalities. We are happiest in our core normal state, or in other words the "You State". If you are not living a life that allows your "you" to shine, you will never reach their true potential. This is the message that is often taught to young people, but as soon as we walk across the stage at our high school graduation, we are expected to conform to some ideal that is laid out for us by society, family or even by ourselves.

Not all of these expectations are bad. My parents expected me to go to college and I am thankful that they expected that of me as education is an important component of happiness. I am speaking of the expectations and pressures of life: getting married, having kids, keeping one job, buying a house, getting a car...The list goes on and on.

The nice thing about our younger years is that throughout our schooling, our mistakes generally don't have high costs. Choose the wrong path in life that is not true to your "you" and the cost is real. In some cases, the cost is hundreds of thousands of dollars real. I recently spoke to a young man who just graduated from law school. He did this with a promise from his father that he would become a partner in his father's law firm once he passed the bar exam. The father paid for school and as promised, upon passing the Bar Exam, my friend was made a partner in the firm. There was only one problem, this young man doesn't like the dog eat dog world of being a lawyer. He feels beholden to his father to stay in the profession because of all that was done for him. I think you can see the issue with this without me going on. This doesn't mean he is destined to serve a life outside of his true calling, it is just a serious detour that is going to require a lot of positioning to get him to where he truly wants to be. Hopefully, this will be a bridge job to get him to his true calling.

Why is being happy so important? When a person is happy, they exude a positive aura. Happy people make great friends, are role models, and they also get the most out of life. Happiness is a mindset. Human relationships with one another and reaching your true potential are the secret to happiness and your happiness is defined by you and only you. Never rely on other people to be the sole foundation for your happiness or to determine what should make you happy. Think of the times in your life that you were the happiest. Think of who was around you, how it smelled, how did you get there, what was the temperature? If you could duplicate this every day of your life, I am sure you wouldn't bat an eye to do so. I guarantee that if you thought about it, it wasn't about money. I'm not saying that it didn't cost money, but it wasn't about money at all.

Happiness is a state of being, and you can feel it in your heart and soul. It is about the present moment, living with a happy you. You have no anxiety, the world is full of promise, stress disappears and you feel like you can do anything. This is a condition that we all strive for and it is priceless. The great thing about life is that just when you think you have things figured out, it all turns in a different direction. Happy people appreciate this shift and embrace the change. I am sure that you have heard the saying that 10% of life is what happens to you, 90% is how you react.

Of course, not all of life is rainbows and unicorns. We all have our ups and downs. There are always challenges like breakups, relationship issues, employment issues, debt (we will talk about this one later) and death, just to name a few. These are all part of the human condition. Regardless of status or position in life, every single person on earth has to deal with these challenges. One of the differentiating factors between those that are happy and those that are not is how they deal with adversity. Remember you must have the valleys to enjoy the peaks of life and the best views come with the most work. Embrace your sadness equally as your happiness. The condition of happiness is always changing with age and circumstance. I love to get older and as I find new perspectives in life, I find my happiness center using my gifts and talents and you can do the same thing. You must figure out what makes you happy.

Here is an exercise to conduct if you are interested. It is called an action board, I met a very successful woman named Karen who constructs an action board every year. She splits the board up into quadrants: personal, relationships, work and home. She then uses cut outs of magazines, quotes, or inspiring words to fill it in. Why spend so much time creating an action board? This becomes a tangible visualization of what you want to do over the next year. You put this in a place that you will see every day to remind you of your path.

CHAPTER 5

HOW TO REDISCOVER YOURSELF?

You may feel like the path to rediscovering your true self sounds very complicated. It very well can be considering your position, but in most cases, it can actually be much easier than you think. First, you have to clear the clutter of your mind. This means unplugging from technology. Now, take some time to examine your life. I know that sounds very serious, deep, challenging, hard and not very fun. This type of examination isn't that bad. Find some quiet space. Go for a walk in the woods, sit by yourself in the park, take a long ride on your motorcycle, find your favorite chair and tune all the background noise out. Examine the happiest times of your life, times when you were at peace with the world. It can be when you were a child, an adult when you first met your spouse or significant other. It could be a location, a moment, a certain environment that you remember. You must quiet your mind and see your life through your own eyes, through your own feelings.

In many cases, the clues lie in your pre-secondary days, a time in which the social pressures were nil. You came home from school, threw your muck boots on and explored a mud puddle. How about a time when you and your friends went on a neighborhood adventure? These valued friends had an unknowing appreciation for your "you". These friendships were based on your personality, not gender, race, socioeconomic status or religion. For me, it was making people smile or laugh.

When we were kids, we were pure. We liked who we liked, what we liked, and did what we wanted to do, regardless of what was normal and abnormal according to our society. People would look at us at this age and say, "Awww, look at that child dressed like a cowboy." Mom would smile and everyone would have a good-natured laugh. There are two little girls in my apartment complex who dress as little princesses. I was taking the garbage out and the two princesses walked past me with their mom. I made the comment to the mom, "I guess we have little princess' today." The mom replied, "Every day." As I began to see them more and more, she was 100% right, the two little girls were princesses every single day of the week. They were happy following their mom on her errands dressed that way and they were cute as the dickens.

Soon this will change for them though and it will be their peers that laugh at them which will force them to convert to being "normal". At some point, they will never put their princess outfits on again.

I was talking to some parents who had a seven-year-old daughter named Holly. Now Holly is a bit of a pistol. One day, the whole family was at church and she asked her parents, "How do you tell someone what they believe is wrong?" This was a deep question and they didn't know how to answer. The parents wanted to give Holly the correct answer as this was a learning point in her life. While they were hemming and hawing about how to answer it, Holly volunteered the information that had her perplexed. She admitted to her parents that her friend did not believe in Santa Claus and she needed to correct her friend's outlook, but didn't want to lose the friendship. Holly was a smart little girl. She believed so much in Santa Claus that she just couldn't understand why her friend didn't and wanted to set her on the right path.

I like to think of this as the Santa Claus Effect. This is the point when we begin to lose ourselves as we shift away from the world of make believe. About this time in our lives, we begin to question the existence of things like Santa Claus, the Tooth Fairy, the Easter Bunny and the Boogie Man. Many times this is initiated by our peers. They use slogans like, "You believe in Santa Claus? You little baby!" This is where we begin to lose ourselves and peer pressure begins to alter our path.

It is amazing what happens between elementary school and high school. As a teacher, I would witness students morphing from wanting to go to school because it is fun, exciting, interesting, and they get to play, to being "too cool for school". In the higher levels of secondary school, the students don't like to joke around, they are more concerned with how they are perceived than with allowing themselves to be a little goofy. The overall pressure is the fear of being judged and ridiculed by the larger peer group. Yet, there is a small percentage of kids who don't really care how they are seen, they tend to fall just a bit outside of normal and yet when they stay true to themselves long enough, they become accepted as who they are. This is done by the "I don't really care what you think" mentality. Their inner "you" is so powerful and they just can't suppress it. This is how I felt when I was in school, I would try as hard as I could to suppress my true self, but after a while, it would always pop out. This isn't to say that I wasn't made fun of, but I think what it did was give me the outward demeanor of "I don't care what you think".

We tend to care about what people think to some degree, but when you know you are a little different, you just accept it and then something magical happens. You graduate high school and that peer group that you were with for twelve years is dissolved. The challenge is that although they are gone, the negative effects still linger.

Those twelve years are probably the most formative years of our lives. Our brain is a sponge; constantly changing, growing, assessing, learning, creating and imagining. Yet when we graduate, we have an average sixty years of our lives left to live, and we still base so much of our own value on our school years. You can see this when people talk about going to their high school reunion. The favorite is the popular athlete who ended up being the hometown drunk and the nerd who became the millionaire. Although I think these are more cliché than reality, they are probably the most popular wishes or beliefs.

I often told my students about this concept. High school social norms, ethics, and values are very narrow, created by what we think high school should be, rather than what it is. For many, high school is a miserable experience with kids constantly comparing themselves to what "normal" should be. I saw this among the poorer students who were unable to afford name brand clothes. Just after Christmas, they would come in with one piece of clothing of the most popular brand. They would wear it proudly as if it was supposed to help them fit. In many cases, that one piece would be worn every single day because it was an outward sign that they were part of the broader concept of accept-ability. It was known that if you wear something that is popular, you will be popular.

The struggle for kids is both real and unfair. We recognize this as adults but in many cases still use these high school standards to judge each other. We cannot choose our family, race, ethnicity, culture, or socio-economic status, yet students are unable to see this and the pressures they place on each other to be normal is enormous. Peer pressure and the desire to fit in can slowly erode one's true self. When students come out the other end of the education machine, in some cases, their "you" is gone. Consumed and altered my peer and societal pressures. Many continue through life without ever returning to their true self.

The same can be said for people who have a high socio-economic status. In their case, they can actually afford to buy the appearance of being popular. The pressure represented here is not from their peers. Instead, the bully is the media machine, which is equally as powerful as peer pressure. It is very easy for people who are able to build up a façade around who they actually are.

With the amount of advertising we see every day through our tablets and smartphones, the pressure is now worse than it ever was. If we have the money, we can buy, wear, and possess whatever the advertisers want. In this mish-mash mix of media control, social control, and pressure, our true selves are hidden under multiple name brand layers. The social approval validates the effort and who doesn't like to be validated? Is mass media having this same effect on your children or even you?

It is important to look at this school-age time of your life because to go back means that you can get into a purer state of mind. As we get older, our ability to experience events and activities changes from its pure state like it does with children. As the saying goes, it becomes harder to see the forest for the trees. We become so involved in the daily grind that we forget to find the simple pleasures. It is never too late to pull yourself out of this trap. It is very possible to get back on the correct path. You are not designed to be miserable that way. You were designed to feel the joys in life. That is why laughing feels so damn good. Revisiting those days will give you a door to explore where your inner you, your inner potential went. The advantage that you have along this journey is the perspective of age given to you by your experiences. Experience allows for purer reflection. This is what I would call the sifting process. With age, social pressure, employment pressures and family pressures, it is very easy to slip away from what you were put on this earth to do. Use these to move back to a path of rediscovery.

Try to find that moment where you actually believed. Forget about the cynics, forget about the naysayers, forget about what you think of the impossible. Reach back, find where the true "you" went, reconnect with it, nurture it, follow it and I promise you, if you live according to that, the rest of your life will be amazing! Choose to begin your journey today, this very moment. Begin to find your path, build your courage, build your confidence, and live an unapologetic life filled with joy, passion, fire and bring those you love along for the ride!

CHAPTER 6

STRUGGLE, FAILURE, AND TRIUMPH: THE LAND OF MEDIOCRITY AND THE LAND OF GREATNESS

Which of these lands would you rather live in? When I talk about greatness, I talk about being remembered for what you have done and who you are. You don't have to be a Steve Jobs or Michael Jordan. I will give you an example of someone who I thought was a great man. His name was Bob and he and his wife owned a cottage on a river in upstate New York. My family used to spend quite a bit of time there when I was growing up. On a recent visit to the cottage, a thought occurred to me as I sat in a chair next to the river. Bob created an environment that valued growth, humor, and freedom. His sense of humor was second to none and it applied to all ages. Sitting there, I realized that I did not have a single negative memory while at his cottage. When I spoke to others about that conclusion, they all concurred. At some point in his life, Bob decided to create an environment of true happiness at his cottage. He did this quietly, humbly and creatively. Bob was living a life true to himself and the positive power he radiated impacted the many people who stayed with him and his wife. He exemplified what greatness is and left an amazing legacy.

So greatness doesn't have to be fame!

The well-known but not often practiced analogy goes something like this:

There are two lands that exist within our society: The Land of Greatness and the Land of Mediocrity. These lands are separated by a mountain called Challenge. The majority of the world lives in the Land of Mediocrity. It is very easy, there is little risk, there is little challenge, and therefore, there is little growth. In this land, there is a lack of personal fulfillment which is often replaced by a longing for something better. In many cases, people here ignore their inner "you". They suppress it, which leads to a manifestation of negative consequences. Eating for comfort, drinking for comfort, prescription medication for comfort, TV for comfort, shopping for comfort... well, you get the point. There is always a feeling of emptiness in the Land of Mediocrity. People here find it easier to sit and be mesmerized and have their actions controlled by consumerism. Because so many people live here, the competition for existence becomes very fierce and in many cases is based on the outward appearance of living. We call this materialism or "keeping up with the Jones'". It is the culture that "if we have, we are happy... if we don't have, we need to get because everyone else has and they are happy and I deserve to be happy". This line of thinking results in debt, stress and unhappiness.

In the Land of Mediocrity, many people long for fulfillment. They want to have an impact on the world. They want to live a spiritual, physical, emotionally healthy, relevant life. It is a deep feeling that rears its head when there is clarity. People in the Land of Mediocrity know that they want to cross into the Land of Greatness because they know what it offers. They crave it but they do not have the courage to turn their desire into reality.

In the Land of Greatness, people are true to who they are. They capitalize on their gifts and talents and they follow their passions. They live a fulfilled happy life that brings those around them up to their level. They leave a lasting legacy and impact on their community, regardless of the size. They are dynamic in their pursuit for fullness in their lives. They take what other people see as risks but know that the rewards are amazing. Those who live in the Land of Greatness have a confidence and know that they can weather the rough times because their foundation is strong. They embrace success and failure equally as an important part of growth. They believe that they are only as good as their last failure. They know that the path is long at times, not instant, but their vision is always with them.

They know that they don't know everything, but are willing to try anything if it makes them better.

These people view the world from an optimistic perspective. They laugh more, have more joy in their soul and their stress is lowered. They live an unapologetic life and don't mind making their own rules or taking a different path. They make it seem easy to those who live in the Land of Mediocrity, but they know it takes a lot of ridicule, judgment, hard work, overcoming challenges, and even sometimes loneliness to get to this land. The People in the Land of Mediocrity are often jealous of those who have crossed over and openly critique them, but on the inside wish they had the courage to do the same thing.

We like to think that these people in the Land of Greatness are rich, powerful, gifted and lucky, but the reality is they are just like everyone else except for one thing, they allow their true "you" to shine. They are who they are and use that to fill their lives with meaning. The Land of Greatness is a state of mind, it exists in the moment, it is powerful, it fuels the soul and the best part is that it is available to you, but only if you are willing to begin the journey.

If the Land of Greatness is so amazing, why are there so many people striving to get there but never arrive? There are two reasons: First, there is a mountain separating these two lands and it is called the Mountain of Challenge. You have to climb the mountain, sometimes blind, knowing it is worth the effort. Secondly, the final step to cross over is one of the most challenging things you will do in your life. I call this "The Precipice" and this is the most difficult part of the journey. Why? Because this is the point you leave the Land of Mediocrity and step into the Land of Greatness. It is at this point that you leave the comfort of the Land of Mediocrity behind. All of a sudden life takes on a new meaning and you become filled with an enormous amount of energy as you allow your "you" to spread its wings as wide as it can and soar. Stepping off the Precipice is a defining moment that is filled with fear, anticipation, excitement, discomfort, power, and self-doubt. It is the point that you take control of your existence, harness the power of choice, and get ready to achieve your full potential.

Let me share with you how I climbed the mountain and when I stepped off The Precipice. This was one of the scariest, invigorating, challenging yet easy, sane and insane moments of my life up to this point.

I ran a small manufacturing business years ago and was caught up in the Great Recession of 2008. We were too small to not fail, so we closed our business and I decided to go back to teaching. I was excited to get out of the entrepreneurial world and into something a little more stable, with less stress and a job that offered retirement. I remember that even at my job interview, I stated that I was looking forward to getting a job that I would be able to spend the rest of my working career in. Teaching was supposed to be that job. I settled down into the public school teacher life and began plodding along. Year after year, showing up to school in

September and leaving in June. I taught history. The problem I encountered while teaching history was that it hasn't changed in 10,000 years. In other words, there wasn't a ton of new material to teach my students and I became bored.

During my seven years as a teacher, I was called into military service on many occasions. At first, my school was supportive, but after a while, they began to grow sick of me leaving and I can't really say that I blamed them. Through training and real world missions, I would get the fulfillment that I was looking for, to be involved in the world again. This is not to say that teaching is not important, quite the contrary. I believe that teachers wield enormous amounts of positive clout with the people that they teach. I was beginning to become aggravated, impatient and unfulfilled. I began to slowly loathe going to school. I found myself bored, frustrated and complaining about a system that I couldn't change.

Two years before I put my resignation letter in I was ready to move on. I toyed with starting different businesses but never really put everything I had into them. I became a cancer in the workplace, constantly undermining my administration's directives because I did not think that they would have any bearing on the current holy grail of teacher assessments, the standardized test. In most cases, the newest, state of the art teaching technique that was being forced on teachers was the same one that was forced on teachers ten years ago that had a new and improved label yet still didn't work.

What I did love about teaching was the positive interactions I had with my students. I would find myself talking about life lessons more than my historic content. What reinforced these lessons even more was the things students remembered from my class. As graduate students, they would thank me for teaching them the straight up reality of adult life that they experienced after they left school. Students wouldn't thank me for my content area, they would thank me for the financial advice or motivational off-topic messages I delivered.

I knew I had to leave but the standard emotions came over me. As I gazed at the Mountain of Challenge and dreamt about the Land of Greatness I was gripped by fear of the unknown, by the "what ifs". My negative mind asked me why I would be so stupid to give up such a stable job to follow my dreams. Of course, this sentiment was echoed by the people I vented to about my job, which reinforced the fears. My insecurities began to take hold. "I am not good enough, I am not talented enough, I will never make it!" "Don't be so stupid", my negative part of my mind would say, "You have it made. Stay at your teaching job, it is comfortable. You only have to be miserable for another twenty-three years, then you can go after what you want...with a pension to boot." Once again this was reinforced by those closest to me. This is what happens in the Land of Mediocrity, it becomes a vicious cycle to stay in your comfort zone. It took me two years to build up the courage and one moment to act on it. So what was the moment I stepped off of the precipice?

It was on February 14, 2016, and it was a spiritual moment, so complex and simple in the same moment that you will only understand when you do this for yourself. It was the moment that I allowed my true-self loose into the world, to live the life that I wanted, unapologetically, passionately and free! I was in a military school in Arizona and it was Presidents' Day Weekend. We were given a four-day pass and I had planned a 1300 mile drive that would take me all over Arizona. This also included fifty-three miles backpacking over the four days. I had asked a few people to go with me. They showed no interest so I ended up going by myself. I packed my backpack, fueled up my car and pointed her north towards the Grand Canyon. My plans consisted of camping under the stars every night, drinking tequila by the fire, and basking in the beauty of the canyonlands.

I had no idea that this trip would change my life.

I met amazing people along the way, and on the second night, I slept on the rim of the Grand Canyon with three Canadian kids, they were only twenty-one. We played cards, drank beer, and we let the sun set over us. They were so full of energy and excitement about life. They had all worked at the same place of employment and hatched a plan where they would all save their money, quit their job at the same time, and travel to the United States first, and then Asia. Their car was old, their equipment was hand-me-down and they existed on Ramen noodles, but their zest for life was incredible. As I was driving to my next destination,

I couldn't help but ask myself why I was not still like that. I had allowed my circumstance to rob my true "you" from being free.

I contemplated this over the next two nights and on the third night I found myself in Sedona, Arizona. I perched on the edge of a tall, three-hundred-foot Mesa, and I had a Valentine's Day dinner by myself. When I spoke to people before my trip about their issues, I had a philosophy. I would help them and offer support as much as possible, but there was a caveat. If they continued to complain about the same thing over and over again without taking action, I would stop listening. I would always say, "Do something about it or shut up!" It was time to take my own advice. As I sat on the edge of the cliff, I had just eaten dinner and was enjoying a little tequila and I witnessed the most amazing sunset of my life. It was at this point when the sun went over the horizon, and the sky went to red, the universe spoke to me, or at least it felt that way. Its words were very simple. "Life is Too Short to Hate Your Job!"

That was it. In a couple of seconds, I decided to take the step.

I resolved that when I returned home, I would resign.

That is exactly what I did.

I knew that I had to quit, gaining the freedom that my true "you" craved and desired. It was remarkably easy to do and I haven't looked back since. It is uncomfortable at times, yes, but I feel completely free, completely happy and completely satisfied that I took that fearful step off of "The Precipice". I am not rich, I am not powerful, I am not a genius but I have the one thing that money can't buy and that is happiness.

Consider this your invitation to join me.

What are the challenges that stand between you and the Land of Greatness? Stop living your life according to what other people think you should be or do. Unleash the true "you" into the world. Are you a cancer in your workplace or your home? Do you bring other people down instead of building them up? Do you have a dream that you want to follow? Your clock is ticking. The Mountain awaits you. Begin your ascent. As you climb, surround yourself with people who want the same thing. Stay away from those who ridicule your dreams and align yourself with those who support them. If they don't understand, point them in the direction of this book to explain what you are doing.

When you reach "The Precipice" step off with the confidence that you have come this far and you are stepping into the first page of the best novel ever written. You are the one that gets to pen the entire thing. Become the author, not the reader. Let the power of your choices bring you to the Land of Greatness. Yes, the way to "The Precipice" will be filled with challenges, and they don't end when you cross over, but they are worth it. Keep your goals in mind and when you reach that destination, let your "you" lead you to places that you never thought possible and bring as many people along on this journey as you can. In doing so, they will begin the climb as well. Leave your mark on the world. Leave a true legacy.

CHAPTER 7

TECHNOLOGY: THE 21ST CENTURY WORLD, WE ARE WHAT WE WATCH

Why have people become so unhappy with their lives? I feel a lot of it has to do with the fact that they live vicariously through other people's experiences, whether on social media or thru television. Over the course of my life, I have struggled to build a life that is not techno-logically or television centered. I spend as little time on social media as possible and do not watch much programmed TV or movies. Adults spend a lot of time in front of the television. Nielsen television ratings put the number hours of television watched by adults at 33 hours per week. That is a total of about 71 days of television per year. If you did this for forty years, you would watch a total of almost 8 years of straight television. No wonder more and more people are increasingly becoming disconnected with the physical world around them and more connected with the cyber world. Television can be a powerful distraction to your path to rediscovering yourself.

Remember that there are thousands of creative people who make a great living writing the words, thoughts, and emotions of those characters that you compare yourself to and that is the design. This has been a slow buildup over the past thirty years, especially with the advancements in video streaming on the internet and the hundreds of cable channels available. All people have to do is sit on a couch, tune their lives out, and focus on the person on the screen, the person doing all the work.

This is often a topic of conversation I have with my grandma. She is in her nineties and uses Skype, Facebook, e-mail, and a cell phone. She has lived through probably one of the most technically developed centuries in human history. When she was a child, she didn't have access to a phone. My grandmother tells the story of when her water broke before the birth of my father, she had to walk to the neighbors in order to get help. There were no computers and indoor plumbing was only in the cities. She often states that it was a simpler time, not necessarily easier, but simpler. People were more emotionally connected. There were not the distractions that we have today. There was no such thing as TV, 24-hour news and mass marketing. Not to mention that marketing to children was virtually non-existent.

Slowly but surely, younger and younger, we are robbing our kids of their internal voice by sitting them in front of the technological babysitter. In some cases, they may never even have the opportunity to develop their true calling because they are so often plugged in. The same Nielsen ratings I wrote about above found that on average children ages 2-11 watch more than 24 hours of television a week. That is almost 3 ½ days of straight television a year or 31 days of television by the time they reach 11 years old. This does not even count video game screen time. Children play outdoors less and less. This is detrimental to their development. Playing outdoors allows the imagination to run free and serves as a conduit for creativity and personal growth. It allows kids to have both success and failure away from supervision in an environment where there are no constraints. There are no levels, on and off switches, or new releases. The same applies to adults. Nature has enormous powers to lift your spirit, clear your brain and get your creative juices flowing. What a great opportunity for you and your family to build deeper relationships, find personal growth and unplug by spending time in the outdoors.

Yes, it is challenging to resist the power of technology. One of the challenges you have is that your inner being can be extremely patient and if you don't allow it to come out, it will sit, waiting for your entire life, never to be released. Every now and then it will say something, but it will be more than happy to allow technology to overshadow its true wish.

We have some significant challenges that we face in the new industrial world where technology advances at what seems like light speed. This occurs all at the expense of the true happiness of our spirits, our hearts, and our minds. It is a reality for all of us on a daily basis, even if you try to resist it. Think about it, we measure the health of our economy around how much money we spend buying gifts for people because that is what we are programmed to do. When I was a kid, Christmas advertising began in December, then the concept of Black Friday came (invented by the producers) and the day after Thanksgiving became the official kickoff to equating love with money. Now we begin to see Christmas ads right after Halloween. In another thirty years, will we begin to see Christmas commercials beginning on the 26th of December?

It isn't just Christmas where we are bombarded with marketing and media which states that we need the newest gadget to make our lives better. The internet is an amazing machine that is used more and more to tell you what is normal and what you need to buy to be normal. To be normal, we are told that we need the newest clothes, the biggest house, the correct weight, and this or that vehicle. The list goes on and on. At some point, we have become immune to the internet following us around, learning our lives and learning just how we search. Remember, multination corporations can collect as much information about us without any restrictions and they do a great job of using it to tell us how to live.

Many people blow these pressures off and do not really believe that it influences them as much as it actually does. I personally try my hardest to be aware of the lures of this type of thinking, but even so, I still find myself drawn toward that mindset. I have to recognize the line of thinking, stop, take a breath and change direction.

Answer the following questions honestly. Are you losing our identity to the social control of technology? Are you allowing outside social media, the internet, and television advertising campaigns to guide your journey? Are you becoming profoundly disconnected from what matters: yourself, your loved ones, and the community in which you live? If you answered yes to any of these, I applaud your honesty. Now, make a choice to change. Make a choice to find your balance.

At the end of the day, your "you" is easily drowned out by all the noise in our busy, fast-paced world and this is not going to change. As a matter of fact, it will only get faster as technology continues to develop. In order to find it, you have to make some very powerful decisions and this concept of "free will" is one of the most powerful personal tools that we possess. Rediscovering yourself is going to take, at the front end, some very profound choices.

CHAPTER 8

DO YOU NEED TO GET RID OF YOUR TELEVISION?

Do you need to get rid of your television? This is a question you should ask yourself. If your palms begin to sweat and your mind tells you that you cannot live without it, then there is a good chance you are addicted. In this case, you may have to take drastic measures. You could give it away, hide the remote three nights a week, you could put your TV in the closet, or even donate it to a school. If you have several televisions that are always on, get rid of them, all but one. This will be incredibly difficult for many people, but it is a necessity if you want to begin to clear the clutter in your brain. Clearing this out will force you to reconnect with yourself and will consequently improve you, your relationships, and your world.

I took a sociology course in 2001 titled *Sociology of the Modern American Family*. The course was a correspondence course and once a month I would have to speak to the professor on the phone. I really enjoyed our conversations as he was a bit eclectic and his view of the world was very unique. One night we had a conversation about technology that still sticks in my brain. The subject was the television itself. He stated that it was one of the worst inventions for humans, ever.

"Bold statement…continue," I said.

He continued, "Although there are some benefits to it, like news, educational programming, etc., it is a go nowhere, hypnotizing nuisance."

"Interesting," I replied. "Do you have an example? This is a very broad blanket statement. How do you figure?"

"Well", he said, "I want you to do an experiment. Have a party at your house and try to get the people into the room with a television. Let the mingling go on for a while and observe people's reactions. Then turn the TV on and observe what happens."

He was correct, that amount of interaction went down quite a bit and people began to turn away from each other and towards the TV. Ok, point to the professor!

"Next." he said, "walk through a subdivision at night and notice the living rooms. Don't look at the television, look at the back wall. Note all the different flickers of light and how rapid the succession is. Almost hypnotic isn't it?"

I did just that, and yes, I believe that he was right. Point two! Of course, these findings are not the most scientific in nature, but sometimes common sense makes for a better theory than the scientific method.

I used to see this a lot with the kids that I taught. Television gives instant gratification, an escape from our existence, and has become one of the best and cheapest babysitters going. I believe that this has had a tremendous impact here in the US and increasingly across the world. TV sucks the years away from us resulting in very little personal growth, it leaves us empty, it takes away our happiness and we begin to live through other fake individuals' lives: their issues, their success, their failures, and we begin to lose our own. Taking away television forces people to engage with their world.

When you scrap the television, at first a level of boredom sinks in, what to do with all that spare time?

How about invest in yourself? Learn something new, choose an art like playing an instrument, learn to draw or paint. What about education? This can be formal or informal as you learn a new skill. Spend time with your family, play games, visit people, build something together, plan a trip. The list can go on and on depending on your interests. Ensure that whatever you do is focused on your personal philosophy of life, you will have more buy-in that way.

I truly believe that in order for you to allow yourself to

come out, this is a hard but necessary step. It can be immensely challenging, but I have not watched TV regularly for years and I still find that I need more hours in the day to go after what pleases me. I do not miss it a tiny bit. I use that time to actually spend with people, cook amazing dinners, exercise, draw, write, paint, or go for a walk. Your mind will beat the haze, the world will become simpler, and clarity will take over. You will begin to see the world as it actually is and you will begin to fall back into what you truly want out of life. It is a process, it is not instant, but represents a necessary sacrifice.

In addition to television, we have the introduction of video games, social media, and internet porn into our society, thereby further complicating and distracting us. These distractions demand that we leverage our power of choice to a greater degree than generations in the past. Let me go back to my teaching days, because kids are a good indicator of where we stand as a society. I witnessed my students completely engaged with video games and staying up until three in the morning drinking energy drinks, then coming to school exhausted in a state where they could not function. I also see people my age (mostly men) doing the same thing. I know two marriages and many relationships that were lost because of gaming and there is now addiction counseling for those with this affliction. An addiction to video games is a waste of time, money, and your life. I am pained to see the effect these electronic games are having on some parts of our society.

I recall a parent teacher meeting I had in which the mother was in tears about how she could not get her son away from the computer (online gaming). He was a bright student but did not perform well in the classroom. I asked her why she didn't take the computer away from her son so he could concentrate on school, which he was failing miserably. She replied that she had tried countless times. Her husband, in his forties and also a gamer, resisted her attempts at restricting their son's playtime. I then asked the son if he would be willing to make a deal. For the following month that I was at the school, I asked if he would agree to not play video games. I explained to him that when men agree on something they shake hands and keep their word. He agreed and gave me his password to his online account. For the next twenty days, he stayed true to his word and as a result his scores and grades began to rise. After one month, he returned to the video games and his grades began to decline once again.

An increasing number of children and adults spend their existence gaming, and many miss out on opportunities in life. The negative impact grows for themselves, their loved ones and their families. Children lose valuable sleep which affects development and growth. They also miss opportunities to learn vital skills for adulthood. Those parents that engage in video games lose precious time with their child which is imperative for their child's development. This time will never be recovered. In many cases, adult males can neglect their spouse's emotional needs as they fall into a technological world that is designed to hook them. This directly results in relationship challenges, and sometimes divorce.

Let me pose this question to you. At the end of the road, when you are lying on your deathbed, will you think back to the TV show that you missed, the level you didn't accomplish on your game, the YouTube video that was suggested on the side list? I would imagine not.

There are so many stimuli that are associated with electronics that at first, a person will go through withdrawal, like that of any other addiction. You must use your power of choice. You can choose to change your life beginning with this choice. Fill the void created by technology with personal growth, learning, creativity, love, feelings, and experiences. Your world will undergo such a powerful transformation as you reconnect with your true self. Your life will be altered for the good. This transformation requires three easy things, at least easy on the surface: choice, effort, and follow through. My personality lends itself to quitting things cold turkey, but you may not work this way. How about constructing a plan to slowly wean you and your family off of technology dependence? Set aside several hours of "unplugged" time every week and fill it with something that encourages growth. Become conscious of when your internet usage becomes unfocused as you follow the rabbit holes of the endless links. This transformation of your mind is not easy. If it was, you would not have bought this book. The fact that you did means that you feel that there is something lacking. Begin to make some of the hard choices to find your balance with technology, refocus your life and begin to feel the inner you stir.

CHAPTER 9

TIME

Time is one of the most critical things at work in our lives. This is especially true considering how little of it we have and you can never buy it, even on credit. Let me share a story about how I came to realize how valuable it is. I feel like I was very lucky to discover this early in my life.

Years ago, I was running a manufacturing business with my amazing ex-wife. When I first began the business with her I was excited to be able to make my own hours, ride motorcycles with my dad, hang out with my grandparents and enjoy the freedom of being an entrepreneur. Boy, was I mistaken. Years later, I was working eighty hours a week, I never really rode motorcycles with my dad, and the business was costing me my relationships with those who were close to me, including my wife.

One day, my ex-wife called me crying. She never cries so I was a little taken aback. I asked her what was wrong. She replied that she thought we were on the wrong track in life. She'd read an email that asked the question: "At the end of your life when you are asked, 'What have you done to make the world a better place?' What would your response be?" I actually took a moment and reflected on that question.

I came to the conclusion that I would not be able to answer that question the way that I wanted to.

Little did I know, but it was at that moment that our lives changed. We ended up selling the business and both contemplated our paths in life. Part of the fallout of this decision was my wife and I separating. Many people were surprised, but we decided that instead of doing the normal thing with a divorce (i.e hating each other) we would value each other. This actually strengthened our relationship and we remain close friends even today. Then I set about on a quest, dedicated to the goal of when someone asked me what I have done for the world, my response will be, "where do you want me to start?"

I am always cognoscente of my use of time. I am always looking to find ways for personal fulfillment in my life (see my Personal Philosophy). Life is about the value that we apply to different aspects of it. As a society, we do not apply the value of time appropriate to its extreme scarcity. It is one of the only things that is unrecoverable. Once used, it is gone, never to return. Yet our lives are getting faster and faster. The pressures of getting everything done exhausts our minds, our bodies, and our spirits. The term running around like a "chicken with its head cut off" is very appropriate to use in this context. The interesting part of the time conundrum is that it is one of the very few things in your existence that you actually have a choice over. It is where you are able to leverage the most power in your life. It is yours, use it wisely. Time is easily squandered. Granted, we all have to work. We have other obligations as well. We always say that we should "make" time for things, but time is not created by a machine. You can't "make" time, you can only choose how you use it.

You and I are both going to die, regardless if you are 18, 28, 38, 48, 98, or 108. My question to you is how do you want to live your seconds, hours, months, years? Will you choose to waste your time or squeeze every second out of life? If you had all the money in the world, you would never be able to buy back time, ever. I have spoken to quite a few successful people (and I mean successful money wise) and they regret that they wasted their time pursuing money; especially at the expense of their relationship with their spouse, friends, and relatives. Use your free will to use your time wisely. Do you want to live in the Land of Mediocrity for the rest of your life, living according to someone else's standard or through media? Or, do you want to live in The Land of Greatness? Choose instead a life lived on your own terms, with the ability to follow your own dreams, flush out your desires, allow your passions to move you into realms of life you never thought accessible.

I ask you to examine your life or the things that you

feel bring you fulfillment and happiness. Make a list of these things and post it somewhere in your house. Do this now. Keep a log of how you use your time during the week. Make a chart of your time use from Sunday through Saturday, don't forget to put your sleeping hours in there. Now examine the list. How much time are you spending on the things that add value to your life and how much time are you spending on frivolous items (internet, social media, Instagram, video games, etc.). I do want to be careful about saying that these things don't add any value to your life, but I think that there is a tradeoff between the two. You have to ask yourself which is more important, spending time with loved ones or watching YouTube. I would argue that one has more weight than the other. At the end of your life, which would you value more, YouTube or relationships? I think that this is a no brainer. As we become more technologically advanced and our distractions increase, this requires all of us to make an even larger concerted effort to use our time in a more productive, fulfilling way.

I find that the more I limit my access to techno-logical distractors, in particular, the internet, which is actually designed to consume our time and attention, my time becomes dedicated to more productive uses. Of course, we live in a world that is programming our brains to work faster, louder, longer, and with more intensity, especially with the ease to which we are able to access media. This requires a sense of self-discipline to avoid being sucked into the media trap. It almost demands that you cut the noise in order to let the true "you" out. By design, media hits the part of our brain that sucks us in like quicksand. You end up on the computer with good intentions then you click on one link or one video, next thing you know, you are hours into the computer and your time has vacated the premises.

Taking time out from social media, television, gaming and the internet will have a profound impact on you. Your mind will quiet much easier. Your stress level will decrease when putting time and effort to tasks that bring about happiness and fulfillment. You will sleep better, your soul will be better, and you will know that you are working towards the ultimate path to the Land of Greatness. Use your time wisely so that when you are asked, "what did you do to make the world a better place?" you can join me and respond, "where do you want me to start?"

CHAPTER 10

CLOSING THE DEBT GAP

Crossing over into the Land of Greatness is more easily said than done and the ease of it can somewhat be a façade, especially as you read the words of this book and I explain to you my experiences and how I got to this point. You may say to yourself, "I can't do this because I have kids, responsibilities, obligations, etc." These often come back to one core foundational issue that plagues our modern industrial, consumer driven society, and it is one word: DEBT. This goes back to the fallacy that to be happy, you must have a lot of money.

When I was a high school teacher, I would always ask my students what they wanted to be when they grew up and almost all of them responded enthusiastically that they wanted to be rich. It has been enculturated in us since a young age that to be successful, you need to be rich. This is not true. Let me switch the subject to prove my point.

Let's talk about investments for a second. Now the word "investment" is often applied to the financial sector, but I like to apply it to the notion of success. In other words, in finding and allowing your "you" to come out. In many circumstances, the greater the success, the harder the work to get there, and the only way that we can assess if someone is successful is to see what is on the outside. There can be a big house, beautiful cars, high paying job, nice clothes, and eating at the best restaurants. What we can't see is what's on the inside. Their soul, their being, where their true self lies. In many cases, the more money you have the more debt you incur, and the more stress penetrates your life.

Some of the happiest, content, and fulfilled people I have met in my life were actually the poorest. This isn't to say that all those who have excess income are not happy and fulfilled or that all poor people are happy, but I want to erase the feeling that the chase of material things is a form of inner satisfaction. I want to change your mindset. I can speak to this myself as I went from a 4000 sq ft house to a 700 sq ft cabin on a lake. This resulted in less stuff, less maintenance, less taxes, and smaller bills. This allowed me to focus on allowing my "you" to develop a lot more because there was less pressure to make the money in order to keep up the previously maintained lifestyle.

When I was advising kids about their future plans, I was often accused of being a "dream stealer" because I would often critique students' college degree choices. I would ask them if they researched the average salary and job outlook, and compare it to the amount of personal debt they would have to incur to achieve a workable degree in that field. More often than not, the student did not do this research. I would do it with them, get the numbers, add interest, then show them the true cost of their degree. Many wanted to go to private schools or schools away from home because they wanted that kind of college experience. What frustrated me, even more, was that the parents hadn't done the research either. I asked what that college experience was, I was curious. It must be really, really good because so many kids were buying into this idea. At the time that this book was written, according to marketwatch.com, the total student loan debt was 1.3 trillion of a 7 trillion dollar national deficit and it was growing by $2726.00 every second. Let me just write that out for you, $1,300,000,000,000.00. I rounded this. That is a lot of zeros.

According to StudentLoanHero.com, a website dedicated to helping students manage their student loans, an average monthly payment for borrowers 20 to 30 years old is $351.00 a month. Get married and that doubles to a $702.00 monthly debt liability. To make it even better, they can never default on their loans...ever. This is an enormous debt liability for young people. What is very scary to myself and many economists is the fact that these young people will have a very hard time building true equity in anything as they age. Especially as they add house debt, car debt, boat debt and consumer debt on top of the pile. Talk about limiting your options to be "you".

Now, not all students go to college for the college experience and I would be wrong if I said that college was a waste of time. It has become quite normal for young people to begin their lives with this much debt. It is also becoming normal for parents to incur debt against their assets in order to help their kids pay for college. This becomes a vicious cycle that in some cases can seem insurmountable to overcome. Let me tie this to the purpose of this book. DEBT IS THE NUMBER ONE REASON WHY PEOPLE ARE UNABLE TO GO AFTER THEIR DREAMS, FOLLOW THEIR PASSIONS, LIVE THE LIFE THEY WANT, AND ALLOW THEIR TRUE SELVES TO SOAR!

I will now deliver amazing financial advice to you for free! Don't Spend Money You Don't Have! We have made it socially acceptable to live our lives with enormous amounts of unneeded debt and this is paralyzing. Debt can be very deceiving, it allows you to present an image on the outside of success, happiness, and satisfaction but it can bury the true "you" so deep that it seems impossible to dig your way out of it. So many times I have spoken to adults who have realized that they need a change in their lives. They say to me, "I hate my job, I am stressed all the time and what I really want to do is such and such, but I have too many bills and too much debt to make the switch." I am sure some of you who are reading this book are thinking the same thing.

There is acceptable debt, typically for a house or your education. Many people have to incur debt for their education and do not have enough money in the bank to buy a house outright. This is fine if done responsibly and with a certain amount of foresight.

If you are reading this book early enough in your life, be smart on how you get your education. If you are reading this book later in your life help mentor those kids getting ready to take on enormous debt for their education. There are so many options out there to get an amazingly low-cost education with grants, scholarships, GI Bill, and community colleges. You will have to do some extra work to get these but the long-term payoff is huge. Before you go to school, research your field to ensure a future pay off. If you need to, wait to go to school until you have discovered your true passion and then go for it. You will enjoy your education more, you will do better in school, and it will be a lot more fun to learn.

If you are reading this book and are burdened with enormous amounts of debt, you can rise out of it. You owe it to your "you" and the rest of your life to do so. Getting out of massive financial debt requires difficult choices and could involve selling your house for a smaller one, selling your car for one with a lesser payment, getting rid of your toys that you don't use that often, going out to eat less and getting rid of cable. Find activities for you and your family to do that are low cost, yet still build better, solid relationships. Use some patience for items that will enhance your growth and your families' growth by using Craigslist to buy gear. Stop shopping to make yourself feel better. Take any extra income, change from underneath the seats of your car, your tax return, sell the jewelry you don't wear anymore, save all of your cans for deposits, clean out your garage and take the metal to a local scrap yard for cash. Take all of this and put it against your debt.

Take ownership of your financial life and this will build an enormous amount of confidence. Little by little, you will climb out of the hole. Buy a finance management book, there are tons available. Your life does not have to turn into an austere one. Make sure you celebrate your small victories by spoiling yourself and your family every now and then but do so within your budget. Just make sure you keep your eye on the prize. Yes, these are all hard choices, but I haven't even hit you with the real biggie, looking for another job. What? "I am already tired!" your "you" will respond. Shut up and do it, there are important things to do with your life.

There is a lot of work and challenges in what I just proposed to you, but you don't have another alternative. There is no magic bullet for getting out of debt except to avoid debt in the first place. This process of getting rid of debt is not an immediate one, it will take time, possibly years and it can be difficult, but I believe you can do it. 1000's have taken on the challenge of overcoming their debt and won. This is one thing you can start working on today.

Time waits for no one and as the great ski film director, Warren Miller, always said, "If you don't do it this year, you will be one year older when you do!"

Begin making the financial choices that will allow you to cross over into the Land of Greatness.

CHAPTER 11

LIFE IS ABOUT POSITIONING

I was camping with my parents and as I walked back to their camper for dinner I hit my head on their awning. My Dad laughed at me as I explained my deep thought to him…" life is about positioning", and I rubbed my head, "and if I had paid attention…to the position of my head….I wouldn't have hit it." But this goes much deeper than banging my head on an awning.

Each one of us has an idea of how we want to live our lives, but this is not going to magically happen. You need to position yourself to follow your dreams, passions, and desires. We are so used to instant gratification that when we think about positioning, we like to think it should be an immediate change. The reality is that it can take years to position yourself to live the life you want. If you start early enough, it can be quicker. If you are in mid-life, it may take a while to clear the debris out of the runway before you can take off.

What does this look like? Well, you need to set a series of goals to get you in the right position. For example, I did not realize the power of positioning until that moment of epiphany that I mentioned above. At forty years old, I began to realize the dream of being free, to let my inner self out of the bag and into the world. How did I do this? Over the past five years, I have made a series of choices that have put me in the right spot. Some of these choices (like quitting my job) were harder than others. By establishing my mindset a few years ago and working towards this moment, I have allowed my dreams to come to fruition.

It is critical to come up with a goal of where you want to be. This goal must be achievable. Then you need to write this goal on a piece of paper, make a poster and place it in a spot that you can always see. Often when we want to achieve a task, we set unrealistic expectations. I found this out when I was running my business. I would put together a very unrealistic to-do list and when I didn't finish it, I would get down on myself.

To remedy this, let me introduce you to something called SMART goals. In 1981 a man by the name of George T. Doran came up with the SMART acronym and applied it to management techniques in the business place. From there, SMART goals have been applied to all aspects of life. Now I am going to apply them to planning your trip up the Mountain of Challenge and off The Precipice. I was introduced to them years ago when I was running my business and have used them ever since, regardless of the tasks, be it personal or business related. Using SMART goal setting ensures that you will be successful in everything you do. They stand for Specific, Measurable, Attainable, Realistic and Timely.

What does this mean? Choose your ultimate goal and break it up into smaller steps. Depending on your goal, you may have to do this over the course of an extended amount of time. It is like building a business. The most successful businesses take years to build and your happy, fulfilled life will take the same amount of time and planning. A successful life is a series of small successes, overcoming a succession of failures with determination and consistency. Commit yourself to a successful life based on your special abilities and talents and I promise you that you will look back on your time on earth with peace and a feeling of satisfaction. This is not applied to just getting out of debt. Apply these smart goals to anything that you need to conquer on your journey to the Land of Greatness. After all, life is often not defined by huge victories, rather a series of smaller ones that continually build on each other.

What does that look like for you? Does it involve downsizing your life; house, car, material items? Does it involve working your way out of debt? Does it involve quitting your job and going after the one you want? How about getting out there to find Mr. or Mrs. Right, or fixing a current destructive relationship with your partner, friends, or family? How about kicking a habit? As you continually go through your transformation you must fill the space of your negative activities in your life by filling them with positive activities. Here is an example. Let's say that you want to quit smoking because it inhibits the lifestyle you want to lead, or it limits your athletic ability or time spent with your kids. If you set your benchmarks to quit, i.e. cutting down the number of cigarettes you smoke per day, what are you going to replace that time that you smoke with? Perhaps you can spend that time writing a book, a journal or a blog. How about outdoor adventures with your significant other or kids, or maybe you learn to play the guitar? If you don't fill that time with something positive, it will become more difficult to make the change.

Let's look at paying down your debt. If you and your family are conditioned to go out to dinner every night and all of a sudden you decide that it is costing too much money, money that could be spent paying down your debt instead. What if with that time, you actually replicated your favorite meal with the help of all the family members? Kids are awesome at doing prep work. Then you sit down and have a family meal. There are a ton of victories in this scenario; kids learning a life skill, more healthy food, more money available to pay off your debt, leftovers for the next day's meal. Most importantly, instead of spending money, you've spent quality time building relationships with your family and your partner.

The key to making theses SMART goals work is to look at all the steps you need to accomplish in getting to the life that you want to live. Before you begin, you must have an end goal. Once you establish your end goal, you have to backwards plan. That means that you have to reverse engineer your life to find out what the steps are that you must take to reach your Precipice. This goal must be what you make your list for and you need to set a relative timeframe…what can you do now, and what do you need to work towards. This is what using your SMART goals to facilitate your change in life may look like:

Immediate (Today): Work on your relationships or get out of a destructive one, research your dream and do a full realistic assessment of how you will get it. Do you need to go back to school, do you need to move, do you need to quit your job, do you need to downsize your life?

Now apply your SMART goal.

Downsize life: Begin with Garage

Specific - Clean out one 20/20 square foot of the corner of my garage

Measurable – 20/20 square foot will be emptied (not re-arranged)

Attainable – Done by the act itself (Action Oriented)

Realistic – Small amount of space given the amount of time and will donate items or list items on Craigslist.

Timely – Spend three hours Sunday afternoon before dinner

When you finish you have achieved a small victory. Make sure you celebrate. Then do the other corner the next weekend. In one month, you have your entire garage cleaned out. Make sure you are focused and you set a reasonable expectation which is the whole key to this process.

You get the point. Setting these goals is going to require time and thought. Make sure you write them down, if you truly want to follow your dreams, this is an imperative step. If you follow my suggestion of unplugging from media and plugging into life, you will have time to do this. If you are in a relationship, the next couple of steps must be discussed with your partner so they will be able to get on board. They might also have some good recommendations for you.

Short Term (Year): Make a map of your year and build SMART goals around your end goal. Some examples may be: get a part time job for the Christmas Season or for the year in order to pay off your credit card bills. Sell your material items and save the money for your switch, begin to prepare a plan for selling your big ticket items and paying down your debt. Begin to focus more time on the "you" that wants to come out. Hopefully, by this point, you have unplugged and are starting to realize how amazing life is when you begin to live it on your own terms. You are beginning to take control of your life. You are realizing the power of choice and how you exercise it. Instead of the light at the end of the tunnel, you begin to just see light. Look back and celebrate your little victories, but also look forward to the amazing things that are about to come.

Long Term (2-5 years) Realistically pick a time that you will be able to make the transition, you should have all major paralyzing debt (credit card, school loans, vehicles) paid off by this point. Plan how much money you will need in your savings account if you plan on quitting your job. If you want to change careers and quit your current job, focus on the moment you are going to resign. Think about how amazing it will be to throw those shackles off and what your plan afterwards is going to be. Your co-workers will be jealous of you because your confidence has built so much, they will be in awe. Others will begin to feed off of your positivity and you will be making a change in the world in which you live. If you want to go back to school to switch professions, if you want to quit your job, if you want to move, if you want to start your business, this is the last phase before you make the leap.

My time came when I had enough money in my savings account. My monthly expenses were reasonable enough that I could afford them with my savings for six months and I was receiving a large bonus from the military. I had positioned myself for this moment, this had been a lifelong goal and I had made the right financial choices and life choices that allowed me to pull the trigger. Of course, as I stood on The Precipice of giving up a very stable job, and with people naysaying and doubting my decision, I had an unbelievable amount of apprehension and fear. But I had come this far, I was ready, this was the moment. I knew that I had to do it. I positioned myself for this exact moment. I was breaking the mold of normal that few ever do, but most should. If I didn't take the step, everything I said, everything I preached, my whole existence would be for naught. And then I stepped..." a journey of a thousand miles begins with one step," this is an old Taoist saying. That is what I did. I stepped off The Precipice and toward the Land of Greatness. People thought I was and probably still feel that I am crazy for doing this simple act. The feeling, power, confidence, and happiness that I felt and continue to feel, I can only try to write it here. You have to experience this for yourself.

Now, how about you? Can you picture yourself at this point? You may argue that you are too old, but age is immaterial. Your true self is wanting out, will you let it? Do you have the drive, patience, and resilience to allow the transformation? Remember that you are never too old to take control of your life and make the impact that your "you" wants to have on the world. Some of the most famous people in America did not get their break or realize their true potential until they were middle-aged or older. Samuel Jackson didn't have his break until *Pulp Fiction*, he was 45 years old. Kathy Bates, *Misery* -42, Morgan Freedman – 52 in *Driving Miss Daisy*. Vera Wang did not start her clothing line until age 40. Gary Heavin opened Curves fitness center when he was 40. Julia Child, a cooking icon, wrote her first cookbook at age 50. Laura Ingalls Wilder did not publish her famous, *Little House on the Prairie* until she was 65 years old and Anna Robert Moses, also known as "Grandma Moses" did not begin to paint seriously until the age of 78.

This is a list of famous people that have "famous" achievements. There are millions of unsung heroes that have achieved a life of fulfillment and satisfaction that have also left a legacy. They may not be household names, but their impact in their sphere of influence is nothing less than impressive. Want to find out who these people are? Begin to ask who highways and bridges are named after, who buildings, schools, parks, or cities are named after. Who scholarships are named after? How about the people who live in the folklore of the family tradition? All of these people crossed over into The Land of Greatness.

Remember, the path is not easy and a real assessment of your life is vital to your success after you make the leap. But if you want it, it is worth it. Kids, debt, responsibilities could make this leap of faith seem daunting. Through planning, preparation, and creative use of your time, resources, energy and capital, you too can make that incredible shift from mundane to exciting, from boring to exhilarating, from mediocrity to greatness.

Position yourself and go for it!

CHAPTER 12

DO YOU HAVE A PERSONAL PHILOSOPHY?

One of the things that has kept me focused and on the path was to come up with my own personal philosophy. This is what wakes me up in the morning and keeps me going when everything seems to be going wrong. It is my foundation. I have made my point that there is enough pressure on us from media, parents, significant others, friends, and society to pigeon hole us into living a certain way or acting a certain way. In many cases, we just go with the flow and do what we think is expected of us. This makes it very difficult to create the circumstance for the true "you" to come out. We fall short of what we think we are supposed to be because of this reasoning. When you allow others to determine your destiny, how can you live a fulfilled, happy, amazing life? The short answer is you can't. Developing a personal philosophy will be your ship in the storm of life, it will anchor you to your true calling and you will need this, often a lot more than others. Many of us have never thought seriously about what our lives should be, or how we should interact with the world, not to mention what our own personal life philosophy should actually be. What I mean by "should be" is written down on paper for you and the world to see. Remember, since our lives are about seasons, your personal philosophy will change a little over time, but it should remain true to who you are.

Time goes by so quickly that before you know it, five, ten, fifteen, twenty years have passed and you feel like you are at the same place as you were many years ago. We end up clinging to the past and our younger selves instead of living the change we want. This is especially true these days with all the plastic surgery, hair growth advertisements, make-up to stay young products and all the hype of remaining youthful. By doing this, we actually miss out on the joy of growing old. You may be reading this book at 18, 38, 58, 78 or 96 years old, just remember that for the most part, your true "you" principles remain the same regardless of where you are in life. You need your personal philosophy to grow. You need to spend time thinking about it, write it down, hone it and redo it until your soul is happy. This will ground you. It is the journey that counts and developing your personal philosophy will act as a spiritual, emotional, and physical road map to the Land of Greatness. Refer to it when you are lost and it will bring you back to the right trail. Sometimes the right trail is longer than others, but nevertheless, it will get you back on the right path

Your personal philosophy should be a simple paragraph, almost like a life mission statement. You apply this every single day you wake up. You even refer to it through times of frustration, boredom, excitement, pain, and the monotonous humdrum of the day in, day out routines of life.

I recommend that you take an hour or two and think about the path that you want to take in the future. Figure out what is the most important thing to you in life (hint: money is not allowed in this equation). Write it down. Use this keyword and begin to develop your personal philosophy around it. Analyze it, play it out, modify it until you feel like you have it figured out. This will be your starting place. Once you have developed a paragraph of your personal philosophy, break it down into four or five keywords. I will share mine with you as an example. This is my homing device to keep myself true in my relationships and for my own soul:

> I want my life to be defined by contributions to the world. I have a finite amount of time on this earth and I am going to use every second of every day to ensure that I become the best human I can be when I die. I will avoid activities and people that don't fulfill or enrich my spirit and embrace activities and individuals that do. Resiliency will be my watchword and my footsteps will always be going forward. I will never quit. I will always make one

more effort. I will live like every day is Friday.

Mantra: Energy, Inspiration, Humor, Nature

You will have to come up with your own. You will need a mantra that defines you and sets your spirit free to enjoy your life and find true happiness. If you are having a hard time, have those closest to you pick some quotes that remind them of your true "you". For example, my parents came home from a vacation and gave me a quote that they feel defined my existence. I didn't think much of it at the moment but thinking about it later, I was honored that they took the time to write it down and give it to me. I like it so much, that I have it tattooed on my arm so that I will always be reminded of it (Note: This, of course, is a radical thing to do and is not a requirement). The quote is as follows: "Live in the present. Launch yourself on every wave. Find eternity in every moment." – Henry David Thoreau

I smile every time I see that quote and it keeps me grounded on my quest through existence. Make your personal philosophy, create your mantra and find a quote. Share this with people along the way, you may be surprised how other people see you, surprised at what you discover along the way and how many people you will bring along with you on your journey.

Applying this philosophy to your life sounds easy, but when the day to day takes over, it becomes challenging to stay true to your chosen path. The reality is our lives as we live them are full of boring, hum-drum, repetitive days. Our relationships with colleagues, friends, significant others, parents, children, and bosses in many cases add a great deal of stress to our lives. We get up, we go to work or school, we do our jobs to our own standard, we come home, we eat, we interact with our family, we plug ourselves into technology, we go to bed and we do it all over again the next day. Throughout the day, we are told by the social forces in our lives that we need something, bigger, better, newer, or different to fill that empty void that begins to build inside of us. In many cases, we look forward to the weekend, the vacation, the holiday, the birthday, or any event that removes us from our reality. Your personal philosophy is your secret weapon against this. It is kryptonite to mediocrity.

You may feel like time is passing you by, that you can't do this. You may feel that there are too many things stacked against you and you don't really feel like you are able to fully apply your philosophy to your life. Many people fall into a depression, take their frustration out on those that they are close to, or turn within themselves. They allow life to dictate how they live as opposed to dictating how they live life. Stay true to your personal philosophy, live by it and it will guide you out of despair. Think of it as your compass. When navigating through the backcountry, people often question their compass and end up getting lost. Do not question your personal philosophy, it will bring you home!

CHAPTER 13

SO WHERE DO YOU GO FROM HERE?

It is my hope that you have found this book useful in understanding how important it is to live life according to your true self. It is perfectly fine to live outside of the realm of what society calls "normal". I hope that you're inspired you to make the changes that you need to set yourself on the path of true fulfillment.

Are you ready? Are you ready to follow your dreams? Are you ready to climb the mountain? Are you ready to take the step off of The Precipice? Do you have the courage, the drive, the intensity to change your life? I can't take you by the hand and walk you down the path. This is a personal journey of growth, self-discovery, and learning. Your confidence will grow with every setback and with every failure that you overcome. Do not be afraid.

Know that this journey will take time and in some

cases, your victories will be so small that you will not think that they are worth celebrating. Celebrate them you must and share them with the world!

I am excited for you and I look forward to your journey. I can't wait to see what amazing things you will do for the world. Your first step is already completed, you finished this book, congratulations!

The rest is on up to you…I will see you in the Land of Greatness and I will welcome you with open arms!

Best Regards,

Andrew

I would love to hear how your journey is going or if you just want to say hello, drop me a line at Andrew@abrechko.com

ABOUT THE AUTHOR

Andrew is dedicated to encouraging people to live a life full of happiness, fulfillment and purpose. Founder of ABrechko Outdoors, a company dedicated to reconnecting people of all ages with the nature, Andrew is passionate about leading a simple life connected to others and the outdoors. Andrew is the *real deal* as his writing is all experience based rather than theory.

Quitting his comfortable job as a High School Teacher to embark on a journey of entrepreneurship and self-discovery, Andrew lives a life with a fundamental believe that *the good life* is achievable by all using the power of personal choice. Follow him on his adventures on his VLOG at www.abrechkooutdoors.com. You can often find him on a river or trail somewhere where the views are epic and the beer is cold.